For Cooper and Riley

Thunder Is Not Scary

Written by
Emily Kahler Rehberg

Illustrated by
Jimmy Chapin and Branden Chapin Craig

On April 27, 2011 a series of storms passed through Alabama. My twins, then two years old, awoke to rounds of rattling thunder around 5:00 am. That day thunder became their fear, preventing sleep and causing tears whenever it was heard. That weekend I searched the Internet and local bookstores for a book to read to them about rain and thunder and lightning, but none could be found that said just what I wanted to say. My husband and I kept saying, "Thunder is not scary." I drew some (very bad) pictures and wrote a brief story on white computer paper held together with a single staple. The story was born. Eventually the boys would tell each other not to be scared, "just like Mommy's book says." Thanks to my husband's persistence, my first children's book was born.

There are many sounds all around us.
Listen!
Can you hear them?
What do you hear?
I hear rumbles.
What could those sounds be?
I hear the rumble of a...

...train!

A train is loud, and it rumbles, but it's not scary.
That's just the sound a train makes when it
chugs on a track.
Chuga, chuga, chuga.

I hear the rumble of a...

...tummy!

A tummy can rumble, and sometimes it's loud, but it's not scary.
That's just the sound a tummy makes when it's hungry and time to eat.
Yum!
I hear the rumble of a...

...truck!

A truck rumbles and it can be loud as it zooms down the highway, but it's not scary.
That's just the sound a truck makes to deliver its cargo.
Zoom!

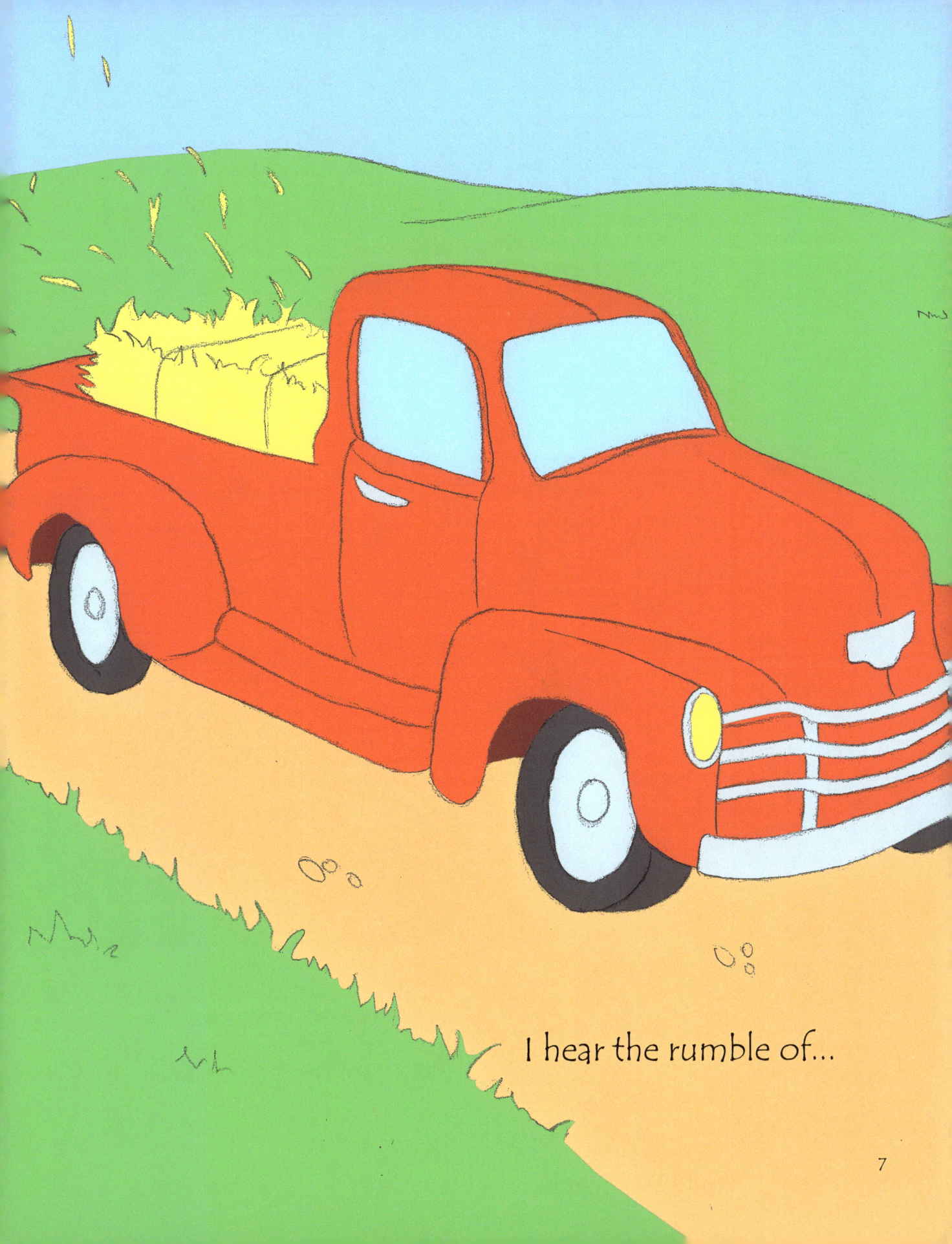

I hear the rumble of...

...Grandpa snoring!

Grandpa snores when he sleeps, and that rumble can be loud!
But it's not scary.
That's just the sound Grandpa makes when he sleeps.
Zzzzzz!

8

I hear the rumble of an...

...airplane!

An airplane rumbles as it takes off to fly.
That can be loud, too.
But it's not scary.

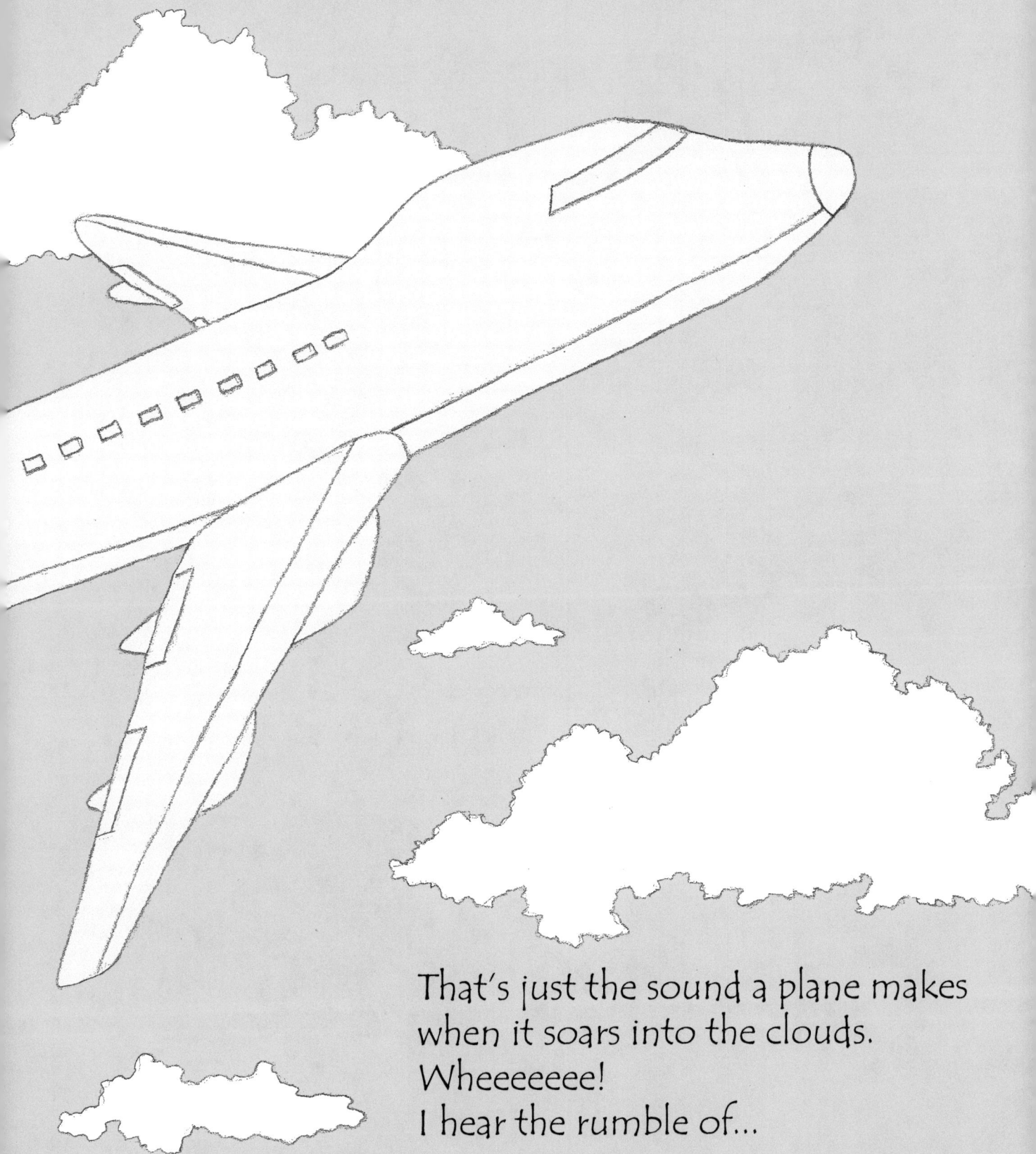

That's just the sound a plane makes
when it soars into the clouds.
Wheeeeeee!
I hear the rumble of...

...thunder!

Thunder is loud and it rumbles.
Sometimes it even makes the house shake.
But it's not scary.
That's just the sound lightning makes when it rains.
Boom!

13

But what would we do
if there was not rain, lightning or thunder?
There would be no water for fish in the pond

or waves in the ocean.

15

There would be no water for flowers to grow

or puddles to splash.

If there were no rain, lightning or thunder,

we wouldn't need rain boots or umbrellas.

So thunder may be loud and it may rumble, but it's not scary!
That's just the sound that rain and lightning make when water gets sprinkled over the earth.

www.ingramcontent.com/pod-product-compliance
Lightning Source LLC
Chambersburg PA
CBHW041558040426
42447CB00002B/223